YOUR KNOWLEDGE HAS

- We will publish your bachelor's and master's thesis, essays and papers

- Your own eBook and book - sold worldwide in all relevant shops

- Earn money with each sale

Upload your text at www.GRIN.com and publish for free

Bibliographic information published by the German National Library:

The German National Library lists this publication in the National Bibliography; detailed bibliographic data are available on the Internet at http://dnb.dnb.de .

Imprint:

Copyright © 2018 GRIN Verlag
Print and binding: Books on Demand GmbH, Norderstedt Germany
ISBN: 9783668779969

This book at GRIN:

https://www.grin.com/document/437828

Robert Komorowsky

Corporate Governance and the new GDPR (General Data Protection Regulation)

GRIN Verlag

GRIN - Your knowledge has value

Since its foundation in 1998, GRIN has specialized in publishing academic texts by students, college teachers and other academics as e-book and printed book. The website www.grin.com is an ideal platform for presenting term papers, final papers, scientific essays, dissertations and specialist books.

Visit us on the internet:

http://www.grin.com/

http://www.facebook.com/grincom

http://www.twitter.com/grin_com

Aalen University

Professorship for Management and Corporate Governance

Emergent Issues in Governance
SS 2018

Corporate Governance and the new GDPR (General Data Protection Regulation)

Author   **Komorowsky, Robert**
                 2nd Semester, Master Business Informatics

Contents

1 Introduction

After nearly five years of intensive work, accompanied with charged political discussions and wide societal echo, the European Union's (EU) Data Protection Reform has finally become a reality. The new framework consists of a General Data Protection Regulation (GDPR), which replaced the former Data Protection Directive, and a new Directive for the police and criminal justice sector. They came into force in May 2016 and will become applicable law as of May 2018. The reform aims at modernizing and harmonizing data protection across the EU and is an essential element of the broader and particularly ambitious Digital Single Market Strategy that the EU launched in parallel and whose far-reaching consequences will unfold in the years to come.[1]

GDPR likely will take on even greater prominence when seen through the lens of the continued fallout created by Facebook and Cambridge Analytica, which have put the protection of customer data in the public eye like never before.[2]

Just a quick reminder: in 2014, Facebook invited users to learn more about their personality type. For this purpose, Facebook used a questionnaire "This is Your Digital Life" developed by Dr. Kogan at Cambridge University. By participating in this survey, 270,000 users may have unintentionally - but allowed under Facebook Terms of Use - shared information about themselves via identity, network and likes with their friends on Facebook. Only when the data was passed on to Cambridge Analytica did Kogan violate the guidelines. These prohibit third party developers from passing on or selling collected data. Almost four years after this violation of the directives took place, the case has recently come to the public by chance.[3]

As this new European Data Protection Regulation will obviously entail many changes for all kinds of companies in the EU and thus Germany, the aim of this seminar paper is to answer the following question: "What measures do German companies have to implement in order to meet the data protection requirements of the new EU GDPR, which is applicable since May 25th 2018?"

---

[1] Cf. Burri/Schär (2016), p. 479-480.
[2] Cf. Kirk (2018), p. 40.
[3] Cf. Gattiker (2018), p. 3-4.

To answer this question, first some important terms that play a role in the regulation are defined (e.g. privacy by design / privacy by default). Then a systematic literature analysis is carried out to identify the most important contents of the GDPR, such as possible penalties for non-compliance. In addition, it will be described how companies outside the EU will be affected by this European legislation.

Next, it will be examined which are the crucial differences of the GDPR compared to the former German *Bundesdatenschutzgesetz* (BDSG), which documentary measures companies must implement as well as which infringements must be reported to supervisory authorities.

Furthermore, the state of sources for this most current topic will be discussed by reviewing the various types of literature (journals, scientific papers, professional service firm literature) used in this seminar paper.

Last but not least, the most important results of this seminar paper are summarised and then, based on these conclusions, four theses are presented and substantiated. Finally an outlook is given on further regulations that are currently in the EU legislative process and will come into effect in the coming years.

2 Terminology

At the beginning of this seminar paper some important terms in connection with the GDPR are to be explained.

Personally identifiable information

Under GDPR, "personal data" is broadly defined to include a person's name, address, phone, e-mail, as well as economic, social, cultural genetic and mental characteristics. Photos, bank details, posts on social networking websites, political opinions, health information, computer IP addresses and more—also are considered personal data. Although the focus may appear to be on data that is captured and stored electronically, in the end, it doesn't matter whether the data is stored electronically on a server or on paper in a filing cabinet. Those holding these types of information now have to obey new, strict rules around transparency and accountability.[4]

Privacy by Design

According to Art. 25 para. 1 GDPR, those responsible are obliged to ensure that data processing systems are as "data-friendly" as possible already during the development and implementation of data processing systems; accordingly, data protection requirements must be taken into account directly in the specification of new products or functions. This also means, e.g. when selecting suitable software in the company, to ensure that the technology meets the latest data protection standards.[5]

Privacy by Default

The "Privacy by Default" stipulated in Art. 25 para. 2 GDPR requires that any default settings for the use of online services or shops be selected in such a way as to work as "data-conservingly" as possible, i.e. only collect such data as is necessary for the respective processing purpose; accordingly, products and functions must already guarantee a high level of data protection for the customer at the first start-up and in the following and if there are different options for data storage or data disclosure, these must be set as restrictively as possible. Only the person concerned can make any changes to the settings if he/she wants to use certain services or functions.[6]

Opening clauses

---

[4] Cf. Kirk (2018), p. 40.
[5] Cf. Schumm (2018), p. 181.
[6] Cf. Schumm (2018), p. 181.

A special feature of the GDPR is that some of the regulations contain so-called "opening clauses". Within this framework, the respective member states - but only in these areas - can make their own regulations, which must then also be applied by the companies. Depending on the location of the company's registered office, these regulations may, of course, contain different or separate data protection regulations of the member states, the knowledge and implementation of which are then also necessary. The German legislator has already reacted to the opening clauses with a law (Data Protection Adaptation and Implementation Act EU – Datenschutz-Anpassungs- und Umsetzungsgesetz EU, DSAnpUG-EU), often referred to as *BDSG-neu* in colloquial language.[7]

---

[7] Cf. Mester (2017), p. 12-13.

3 Fundamentals of the EU GDPR

One difference from the existing law that is evident without a closer look at the legal texts is that the new data protection rules are framed in a regulation, as opposed to the previously used instrument of the directive. While both types of EU legal acts can in principle ensure a high level of harmonization across the member states, a regulation is directly applicable and does not require additional domestic implementation (whereas a directive defines the results to be achieved leaving the choice of the means for achieving them up to the member states). Moreover, regulations immediately become part of a national legal system, have a legal effect independent of national law, and override contrary national laws. Overall, this guarantees a higher level of harmonization and fewer differences across member states—also disciplining certain member states, such as Ireland, for their rather mild enforcement of data protection rules (notably vis-à-vis Facebook).[8]

3.1 Contents of the EU GDPR

The purpose of the GDPR is to protect the personality and fundamental rights of persons whose data are processed. In principle, the GDPR means that persons now have these six important rights in the area of data protection:

1. right to information about which data is stored

2. right to object to the processing of personal data, for example in direct marketing

3. right to be forgotten, i.e. the deletion of one's own data

4. right to data transferability, i.e. transfer of own data to third parties

5. right to a complete and comprehensible data protection declaration

6. right to information within 72 hours in the event of a data breakdown, for example due to hacker attacks.

Both natural and legal persons are covered by the protection area. The term "processing" refers to any handling of personal data - from collection to archiving and destruction.[9]

Perhaps the most hotly discussed change is the introduction of a "right to be forgotten" by virtue of Article 17 GDPR. The latter extends the existing right under Article

---

[8] Cf. Burri/Schär (2016), p. 489.
[9] Cf. Gattiker (2018), p. 3.

12(b) of the Data Protection Directive's "right of erasure." In particular, a data subject can now have her personal data erased and no longer processed, where the data is no longer necessary in relation to the purposes for which it was collected; where a data subject has withdrawn her consent or objects to the processing of personal data concerning her; or where the processing of her personal data is otherwise contrary to the Regulation.[10]

Lastly, companies operating in several EU member states will no longer have to deal with the individual national data protection authorities in all these countries (as was the case before the Regulation came into effect). Instead, the supervisory authority of the member state of the registered office or the main branch will be the competent authority for the company (so-called "one-stop-shop mechanism").[11]

3.2 Extended range of sanctions

Art. 43 para. 3 sentence 1 BDSG has so far provided for fines of up to EUR 50,000 and up to EUR 300,000. Article 83 GDPR now provides for far higher fines. For companies, the fine can amount to up to EUR 20 million or up to 4% of global sales, whichever is higher (Art. 83 para. 5 GDPR). Certain violations mentioned in Art. 83 para. 4 GDPR, in particular data security pursuant to Art. 32 GDPR, are punishable by fines of up to 2% of sales; until now, such violations were not punishable by fines pursuant to § 9 BDSG. Individuals are liable to fines of up to €20 million.[12]

The respective amount of the fine is at the discretion of the authority. However, it must be guided in its decision by "discretionary factors". For example, the authority has to consider how serious the infringement is and how many persons are affected by it, whether the infringement was committed intentionally or negligently or also whether it is a repeated infringement, cf. Article 83 paragraph 2 GDPR.[13]

It should be noted that in addition to this general rule, another provision of the GDPR allows member states to lay down the rules for other penalties that would be applicable to infringements of the GDPR that are not subject to the pre-defined administrative fines.[14]

---

[10] Cf. Burri/Schär (2016), p. 490.
[11] Cf. Koch/Schmidt-Seidl (2016), p. 72-73.
[12] Cf. Schumm (2018), p. 183.
[13] Cf. Koch/Schmidt-Seidl (2016), p. 77.
[14] Cf. Gilbert (2016), p. 7.

3.3 Relevance for countries outside the EU

The GDPR applies not only to companies based in Europe, but to all companies of-fering goods or services within the EU. As a result, companies established outside the EU must also comply with the new data protection regulations if they are active in EU member states and process personal data collected there. This is called the "marketplace principle".[15]

As businesses do not have to be located in the EU to fall under GDPR, the law im-pacts every business that markets and sells goods or services to EU residents online or holds personal data of EU citizens, even if the business has no physical presence in the EU. So that means if a company has no offices or staff in any EU country, and even no customers in the EU, but it in any way processes and stores personal data on EU residents or customers, it falls under the jurisdiction of GDPR. In short, if an organization does any business with the EU or with EU consumers, GDPR most like-ly will apply.[16]

---

[15] Cf. Koch/Schmidt-Seidl (2016), p. 72.
[16] Cf. Kirk (2018), p. 41.

4 Effects of the EU GDPR on German companies

4.1 Crucial differences to the former *Bundesdatenschutzgesetz* (BDSG)

4.1.1 *Increased reporting obligations*

The main objective of the new GDPR is to create transparency vis-à-vis the person concerned by regulating new information obligations. The data subject should be informed about which data are processed in the company and for what purpose.[17]

The information obligations were therefore significantly extended by Art. 12 to 15 GDPR. Now, according to Art. 13 GDPR, the following information must be provided at least and in part new:

- name and contact details of the person responsible and (new) their representative, if applicable
- (new) if necessary, the contact details of the data protection officer
- purposes of data processing
- (new) legal basis for processing
- (new) duration of data storage or the criteria for determining this duration
- (new) the existence of a right of access, rectification, deletion or limitation of processing or opposition and of the right to data transferability
- (new) the existence of a right of appeal to a supervisory authority
- (new) whether the provision of the data is required by law or contract or necessary for the conclusion of a contract, whether the user concerned is obliged to provide the data and what consequences it has if he does not comply
- (new) if processing is based on consent, the existence of a right of withdrawal.[18]

4.1.2 *Extended rights of objection*

According to the GDPR, data subjects may at any time object to the processing of personal data concerning them, which is based on Art. 6 para. 1e or f GDPR. If data have been collected "lawfully" in accordance with one of these two conditions, the data subject may at any time object to the processing of such data, even though the collection of the data was lawful. The objection pursuant to Art. 21 para. 1 sentence 1

---

[17] Cf. Koch/Schmidt-Seidl (2016), p. 74.
[18] Cf. Schumm (2018), p. 179-180.

GDPR leads to a processing prohibition with regard to the data concerned; companies may therefore no longer use these data in principle. However, the data controller has the right to process the data concerned, in exceptional cases, if there are compelling reasons worthy of protection (above all economic reasons) for further processing or if the company aims to defend legal claims.[19]

While until now it has only been mandatory to refer to the possibility of revocation with effect for the future in the case of electronic consents, this information will always be required since 25 May 2018. The purpose of this is to remind the person concerned that their consent is voluntary. And the revocability expresses this voluntariness for the future.[20]

4.1.3 Right to be forgotten

Another new principle of the GDPR is the so-called "right to be forgotten". Thus, the obligation to delete acc. to Art. 17 para. 1 GDPR is extended in comparison with the previous § 35 para. 2 sentences 2 and 3 BDSG. In the following cases, the data subject now has the right to demand that his or her data be deleted:

- the data is no longer required for the original purposes
- revocation of consent in the absence of another legal basis for data processing
- in principle in the event of an objection to processing pursuant to Art. 21 para. 1 GDPR
- opposition to the use of the data for direct marketing purposes
- unlawfulness of the processing
- legal obligation to deletion under Union law or national law
- processing on the basis of consent to the processing of children's data.

21

4.1.4 Right to Data Transferability

Under the right to "data transferability", under Article 20(1) of the GDPR, the data subject is entitled to the surrender of personal data that he or she has provided to the

---

[19] Cf. Schürmann (2017), p. 150-151.
[20] Cf. Kramer (2016a), p. 207.
[21] Cf. Schumm (2018), p. 181.

company. However, the right to surrender exists only in the case of data processing which is based on the consent of the data subject or on processing for contractual purposes. Another prerequisite is automatic processing. If these conditions are met, the data subject must on request be provided with all personal data which he has provided to the controller in a structured, common and machine-readable format. If this is technically feasible, the data subject may also request that the data be transferred directly from one responsible body to another (Article 20(2) GDPR).[22]

4.1.5 Changes in age restrictions

The GDPR also addresses the special case of children. For e-commerce, social media, content, or information service providers to process personal data of persons younger than 16 years, the consent of the child's parent or custodian will be required. This is a case where the rule will differ from Member State to Member State. Since this is one of the many opening clauses, the GDPR allows Member States to lower this age limit to 13 years.[23]

4.2 Documentation requirements

Another important element of the new regulations are the documentation requirements laid down in various parts of the regulation. In particular, these should enable the respective data protection supervisory authorities to check the legality of the data processing operations in the company. Documentation obligations now exist in the following areas, among others:

- Articles 24 and 28 GDPR: Documentation of processing operations of data controllers and data processors,
- Article 30 GDPR: Records of processing activities
- Article 33(5) GDPR: Documentation of "data breaches",
- Article 35 GDPR: Data protection impact assessment,
- Article 47 GDPR: Documentation suitable for third country guarantees

[24]

A "record of processing activities" has to include specified information such as the purpose of the processing, the categories of data and data subjects, the categories of

---

[22] Cf. Koch/Schmidt-Seidl (2016), p. 75-76.
[23] Cf. Gilbert (2016), p. 6.
[24] Cf. Koch/Schmidt-Seidl (2016), p. 76.

recipients to whom the data will be disclosed, including recipients in third countries or international organizations, and the envisaged time limit for the erasure of the different categories of data. Companies are expected to keep records of transfers of personal data to a third country, and the documentation of the appropriate safeguard to legitimize the transfer, as well.[25]

Another change results from the fact that according to the GDPR the record of processing activities only needs to be created if the company/organization has at least 250 employees. In the past, this was already the case from ten employees. However, there are also exceptions: if the company/organisation processes

(a) data presenting risks to the rights and freedoms of data subjects,

(b) in particular sensitive data; or

(c) personal data relating to criminal convictions; or

(d) if data processing is continuous,

companies /institutions with fewer than 250 employees must also compile a record of processing activities.[26]

Finally the GDPR specifies that the responsible person, thus the management, has to keep a list of all processing activities instead of the data protection commissioner. The data protection officer of a company can continue to provide this - but now the management will be liable for this.[27]

Furthermore, Article 35 GDPR stipulates that all companies must now carry out a so-called "data protection impact assessment" for data processing processes that involve a "high risk" for those affected (risk-based approach). Among other things, profiling processes, the processing of health data and the processing of racial data are considered risky in this sense. In addition to the impact assessment, in the case of particularly risky processing operations, consumer associations must even be consulted (Article 35(9) GDPR) or a notification procedure to the appropriate data protection supervisory authority (Article 36 GDPR) is to be performed.[28]

The content of an impact assessment is regulated in Art. 35 para. 7 GDPR and includes e.g.

---

[25] Cf. Gilbert (2016), p. 6.
[26] Cf. Kramer (2016b), p. 103.
[27] Cf. Philipp (2018), p. 1.
[28] Cf. Koch/Schmidt-Seidl (2016), p. 76-77.

a systematic description of the planned operations and purposes of the processing, an assessment of necessity and proportionality in relation to the purpose

an assessment of the risks to the rights and freedoms of those concerned, and the planned remedial measures and safety precautions.

29

4.3 Violations to be reported

Like § 42a BDSG, the GDPR also contains regulations on the duty to provide information in the event of "data protection breaches". Articles 33 and 34 GDPR distinguish in this respect between a notification to the supervisory authority and a notification to the person concerned. The supervisory authority must be informed within 72 hours if the rights of the persons concerned are affected.[30]

The supervisory authority shall then be informed of the following:

a description of the nature of the breach, where possible indicating the category of data and the approximate number of personal data records concerned

the name and contact address of the data protection officer

a description of the probable consequences

a description of the measures taken or proposed to remedy the data protection breach and, if necessary, measures to mitigate the possible effects.

31

If the data breach is likely to result in a "high risk to the rights and freedoms of individuals", the controller also will be required to inform the data subjects without undue delay of the occurrence of the breach unless an exception applies. If a data controller fails to notify the affected individuals, the supervisory authority may require the data controller to do so, or may decide that an exception applies.[32]

In the case of international organisations, the data protection supervisory authority in whose country the organisation has its headquarters in the EU ("lead supervisory authority") is competent. The persons concerned may contact the nearest superviso-

---

[29] Cf. Schumm (2018), p. 179.
[30] Cf. Koch/Schmidt-Seidl (2016), p. 77.
[31] Cf. Schumm (2018), p. 181-182.
[32] Cf. Gilbert (2016), p. 7.

ry authority, which must then pass the matter on to the supervisory authority concerned; it is therefore irrelevant where the infringement occurs ("one-stop-shop principle "). Companies only need to work with the data protection authority that is responsible for them at headquarters. The supervisory authorities themselves must coordinate their activities.[33]

---

[33] Cf. Schumm (2018), p. 182.

5 Literature analysis

5.1 Systematic Literature Analysis

The next section describes how the process of literature research to answer the re-search question of this seminar work was conducted.

First four databases from the economics sector were selected, and then searched for suitable sources. The following were picked:

- Business Source Premier (via *EBSCOhost*), an important research database for the economic sciences
- *EconBiz*, a virtual library for economics and business studies
- *JSTOR*, a digital library with access to more than 12 million academic journal articles, books, and primary sources
- *WISO*, a licensed database for economic and social sciences.

In order to find suitable sources, the following systematic actions were carried out: to begin with, two constructs A and B were defined (A: "EU-GDPR" and B: "impact") and several German and English synonyms were identified for each construct. These were:

- For A: „GDPR", „DSGVO"
- For B: „consequences", „changes", „Auswirkung*", „Folge*", „Änderung*", „An-forderung*", „Sanktion*", „Haftung*", „Umsetzung*"

Next, all possible combinations of the synonyms of construct A and B were formed (e.g. "DSGVO" AND "Anforderung") and each of the four databases was searched with these combined search terms. To increase the number of search results, they were also searched individually for the terms "GDPR" and "DSGVO".

To specify the search results, the following search criteria were used:

- Publication date: 2016 to 2018
- Language: English, German
- Document type: article
- Publication type: Academic Journal

All in all, this systematic literature research yielded 118 results (ECONIS: 15, JSTOR: 13, EBSCO: 22, WISO: 68). The WISO database thus delivered by far the most hits.

From this resulting paper summary model, first the duplicates were removed, and then those sources, which already indicated by their title and their abstract that they had nothing to do with the problem statement. Through this manner, only 42 possible sources remained.

These sources were exported directly from the respective database into the literature management program Citavi and then searched more precisely to find the titles that could be used to answer the research question. In this way, only 10 suitable sources remained. These were mainly consulting literature (e.g. from specialized lawyers) or articles in professional journals in the fields of IT and data protection. Since the GDPR was not yet applicable at the time of the literature search, there was understandably not very much scientific literature dealing with the effects of the regulation.

The following is a brief description of the most important sources found in the context of systematic literature research. It is limited to the sources cited at least three times in this paper:

- Mira Burri and Rahel Schär (2016): The Reform of the EU Data Protection Framework. Outlining Key Changes and Assessing Their Fitness for a Data-Driven Economy (article in *Journal of Information Policy*). This article describes the key changes by the GDPR, especially with regard to cross-border flow of data.
- Gilbert, Francoise (2016): EU GENERAL DATA PROTECTION REGULATION: WHAT IMPACT FOR BUSINESSES ESTABLISHED OUTSIDE THE EUROPEAN UNION (contribution in *Journal of Internet Law*). This article discusses the GDPR and addresses in particular the export of personal data outside the EU.
- Kirk, Nancye (2018): Compliance and Personal Data Protection (article in *Journal of Property Management*). The article discusses how foreign businesses can fall under jurisdiction of GDPR as well as the concepts consent, right to be forgotten and access to data.

5.2 Additional Literature

Another important article describing the effects of GDPR is the following:

- Gattiker, Urs (2018): EU-Datenschutzgrundverordnung (DSGVO): Was ist Sache für Marketing-Manager, Geschäftsleitung und Vorstand (whitepaper by *Deutscher Marketing Verband (DMV) des Competence Circles Digital Market-*

places). This article points out the most important changes by the GDPR to which enterprises have to adjust as well as links to further resources on the topic.

5.3 Professional Service Firms

Finally, articles of professional service firms that have been researched in the WISO database will be described. Many of the journal articles refer only to special application areas of the GDPR, e.g. scoring procedures, data processing in hospitals or of cloud providers. These sources were not further investigated in this seminar paper. Nevertheless, the research also revealed professional service literature, which described the general requirements of the GDPR. The most important of them were:

- Koch, Christian and Schmidt-Seidl, Jan (2016): Europäischer Datenschutz. Neuer Wein in alten Schläuchen? (article in *BankInformation*). This article gives a good overview of the changes of the GDPR compared to the BDSG.
- Philipp, Martin (2018): 6 To-dos für rechtskonformes Lead Management und E-Mail-Marketing (article in *marconomy – das Fachportal für B2B Marketing und Kommunikation*). This article provides useful instructions for ensuring the legal conformity of email marketing processes in accordance with the GDPR.
- Schumm, Harald (2018): Die Datenschutz-Grundverordnung im Unternehmen (*Schumm & Aigner GmbH Rechtsanwaltsgesellschaft Wirtschaftsprüfungsgesellschaft, Nürnberg*, article in *StuB - Unternehmenssteuern und Bilanzen*). This contribution gives a quick and uncomplicated overview about the process adjustments in the enterprise that are necessary by the GDPR.

As can be seen from the description of the sources, English-speaking publications mainly deal with questions on how to deal with data originating in the EU but that are processed in non-European countries. This is probably due to the fact that the GDPR explicitly regulates that all companies that process personal data of European customers must comply with the regulation, regardless of whether a company has a registered office in the EU or not.

German-language sources, on the other hand, tend to deal with questions relating to the concrete implementation of the GDPR. Above all, it is about how companies have to change their business operations in order to meet the requirements of the GDPR, which are not particularly specific, with the goal of not having to expose themselves to the risk of expensive fines.

6 Conclusion

Probably the most important changes by the GDPR for German companies result from the increased documentation requirements, in particular from the record of processing activities and the data protection impact assessment. Companies must now be able to prove at any time that their processes comply with data protection regulations. This is equivalent to a reversal of the burden of proof, which is why especially for small and medium-sized enterprises an increased consulting effort is necessary, which must then be purchased by external data protection consultants.

In the course of preparation for the GDPR, companies therefore had to obtain numerous consents from customers, employees, business partners and suppliers so that they could continue to process their data. Also, numerous data protection declarations had to be modified and standardized throughout Europe, which explained why the term GDPR came across in the spring of 2018 virtually every day, both for employees in companies and private individuals.

Furthermore, according to GDPR data breaches must now be reported to the relevant data protection authorities much faster (within 72 hours) and their consequences described in data protection impact assessments.

In addition, another important organizational requirement arises from the fact that companies now have to be able to hand over data about their customers at any time and, if they so wish, delete it immediately ("right to be forgotten"). Also enterprises are now required to be technically capable of publishing their customers' data in a machine-readable format so that customers can easily transfer their data to other companies.

Last but not least, companies are now exposed to an increased liability risk, which is a consequence of the very sharply increased fines (20 million euros or 4% of the worldwide annual turnover). This resulted in a great deal of uncertainty, especially among many small and medium-sized enterprises.

All in all, the GDPR leads to considerable changes for companies in Germany. For this reason, four theses are now to be formulated which can be derived from the results of this seminar paper.

- **Thesis 1:** *Due to the GDPR, for German companies there are no fundamental changes in data protection law compared to the BDSG.*

However, there is a considerably higher implementation effort, for example with regard to the documentation of data processing operations. This is primarily due to the fact that fundamental principles of data protection, as regulated in the BDSG or UWG, were retained in the GDPR and Germany had already demonstrated a high level of data protection compared to other European countries. On the other hand, the bureaucratic effort due to the GDPR is higher, for example due to stricter documentation requirements. Of course, this involves comparatively higher costs for smaller companies than for large companies. For this reason it can also be concluded that many fears that German companies had before the GDPR came into force and were exaggerated in the media are partly unfounded.

- **Thesis 2:** *German companies are not yet sufficiently prepared for the GDPR.*

Although the contents of the GDPR are known since the regulation came into effect in 2016, many German companies, especially small and medium-sized ones, were not ready in time to implement all requirements of the regulation by the end of the deadline and will continue to be busy implementing them after 25 May 2018.

- **Thesis 3:** *The European legislator did not sufficiently consider the practical implementation in enterprises when formulating the GDPR.*

Due to the high complexity of the GDPR it is obvious that many of its requirements are only insufficiently implemented in practice, since the control of the compliance with the regulation is hardly possible despite all documentation obligation. The associated legal uncertainty, such as how strictly the supervisory authorities impose fines or initially only issue reprimands, means that many companies need more professional advice and thus have to invest more money in external consultants and training for their own employees. Large data processing companies such as Facebook or Apple, which should have been taken to the curb by the GDPR, can obviously afford this much easier compared to small and medium-sized enterprises, which have already been relatively secure with customer data and were comparatively little involved in data scandals such as *Cambridge Analytica.*

By the way, a further consequence of the unclear regulations of the GDPR is that even warning associations do not know clearly what stands behind many of its regulations. This also means that the huge wave of warning notices feared by many German companies following 25 May 2018 has failed to transpire for the time being.

- **Thesis 4:** *The increased sensitivity to data generated by the GDPR means that the EU is falling behind on innovative technologies.*

Stricter data processing rules may suggest that companies in the EU will be more reluctant to develop new and innovative products or business models based on big data in the future such as artificial intelligence. Autonomous driving, for example, requires a great deal of data to learn how to drive independently and how to avoid accidents. The constant retrieval of declarations of consent now unnecessarily restricts the efficiency of data processing. It is also difficult to imagine a right to erasure with the blockchain, i.e. a constantly growing, unerasable data set on which e.g. crypto currencies such as Bitcoin are based. The GDPR guidelines thus make data-driven innovations considerably more difficult, which is probably another reason why the EU will continue to lag significantly behind countries such as the USA or China, where data protection regulations are far less strict.

However, the GDPR is only the beginning of new data protection regulations: the EU is currently working on an even more far-reaching *e-privacy regulation*, which will regulate almost every form of electronic communication from 2020 onward at the earliest.

Another example of the EU restricting the internet is the *EU copyright reform* that will oblige online platforms with user-generated content (e.g. YouTube, Facebook) to take "appropriate and proportionate measures" to prevent the distribution of unlicensed works. In future, this will only be possible through so-called upload filters, even if this is not explicitly stipulated in the legal text.

7 Bibliography

Burri, Mira/Schär, Rahel (2016)

The Reform of the EU Data Protection Framework: Outlining Key Changes and Assessing Their Fitness for a Data-Driven Economy, in: Journal of Information Policy, Vol. 6., p. 479–511

Gattiker, Urs (2018)

EU-Datenschutzgrundverordnung (DSGVO). Was ist Sache für Marketing-Manager, Geschäftsleitung und Vorstand?, in: Absatzwirtschaft, Nr. 01/02, p. 1–12

Gilbert, Francoise (2016)

EU GENERAL DATA PROTECTION REGULATION: WHAT IMPACT FOR BUSINESSES ESTABLISHED OUTSIDE THE EUROPEAN UNION, in: Journal of Internet Law, Vol. 19, Nr. 11, p. 3–8

Kirk, Nancye (2018)

Compliance and Personal Data Protection, in: Journal of Property Management, Vol. 83, Nr. 3, p. 40–41

Koch, Christian/Schmidt-Seidl, Jan (2016)

Neuer Wein in alten Schläuchen?, in: BankInformation, Nr. 08, p. 72–77

Kramer, Philipp (2016a)

EU-DSGVO: Einwilligungserklärung im Übergang, in: Datenschutz-Berater, Nr. 10, p. 206–207

Kramer, Philipp (2016b)

EU-Recht: Neues Verfahrensverzeichnis nach EU-DSGVO, in: Datenschutz-Berater, Nr. 05, p. 103

Mester, Britta A. (2017)

Auswirkungen der DSGVO auf die IT, in: Wirtschaftsinformatik & Management, Vol. 9, Nr. 4, p. 12–15

Philipp, Martin (2018)

EU-DSGVO. 6 To-dos für rechtskonformes Lead Management und E-Mail-Marketing, in: marconomy.de

Schumm, Harald (2018)

Die Datenschutz-Grundverordnung im Unternehmen, in: StuB - Unternehmenssteuern und Bilanzen, Nr. 5, p. 177–183

Schürmann, Kathrin (2017)

Die Widerspruchsrechte in der DSGVO, in: Datenschutz-Berater, Nr. 07-08, p. 150–151